Russian Littoral Submarines & Submersibles

Piranha/Piranha-T/P-550/P-650E/Triton-I/II, Rus & Bester

Hugh Harkins

Copyright © 2019 Hugh Harkins

All rights reserved.

ISBN: 1-903630-83-5
ISBN-13: 978-1-903630-83-9

Russian Littoral Submarines & Submersibles

Piranha/Piranha-T/P-550/P-650E/Triton-I/II/Rus & Bester

© Hugh Harkins 2019

Published by Centurion Publishing
United Kingdom

ISBN 10: 1-903630-83-5
ISBN 13: 978-1-903630-83-9

This volume first published in 2019

The Author is identified as the copyright holder of this work under sections 77 and 78 of the Copyright Designs and Patents Act 1988

Cover design © Centurion Publishing & KDP

Page layout, concept and design © Centurion Publishing

All rights reserved. No part of this publication may be reproduced, stored in a retrieval system, transmitted in any form, or by any means, electronic, mechanical or photocopied, recorded or otherwise, without the written permission of the publisher

The publisher and author would like to thank all organisations and services for their assistance and contributions in the preparation of this volume: 33 Shipyard (33CPE); CDB ME-Rubin (Central Design Bureau for Marine Engineering, Rubin); JSC Admiralty Shipyards; JSC Almaz Central Marine Design Bureau; JSC Avora Scientific and Production Association; JSC Bars; JSC CDB Lazurit; JSC Concern CSRI Elektropribor, State Research Centre of the Russian Federation; JSC Concern Okeanpribor (Oceanpribor); JSC Experimental Machine Design Bureau, Novator; Malachite SPB JSC (The St. Petersburg's Sea Bureau of Mechanical Engineering, 'Malachite'); Ministry of Defence of the Russian Federation; PJSC Plant Red Sormovo (Krsormovo); Rosoboronexport; United Shipbuilding Corporation; US DoD/DIA

CITATION GUIDE: 33CPE (33 Shipyard); CDB ME-Rubin (Central Design Bureau for Marine Engineering, Rubin); Admiralty (JSC Admiralty Shipyards); Almaz (JSC Almaz Central Marine Design Bureau); Avora (JSC Avora Scientific and Production Association); Bars (JSC Bars); CDB Lazurit (JSC CDB Lazurit); Elektropribor (JSC Concern CSRI Elektropribor, State Research Centre of the Russian Federation); Oceanpribor (JSC Concern Okeanpribor (Oceanpribor); Novator (JSC Experimental Machine Design Bureau, Novator); Malachite (Malachite SPB JSC (The St. Petersburg's Sea Bureau of Mechanical Engineering, 'Malachite'); MODRF (Ministry of Defence of the Russian Federation); Krsormovo (PJSC Plant Red Sormovo (Krsormovo)); Rosoboronexport (Rosoboronexport); USC (United Shipbuilding Corporation)

CONTENTS

	INTRODUCTION	vii
1	RUSSIAN/SOVIET LITTORAL SUBMARINE, MIDGET SUBMARINE & SUBMERSIBLE DESIGN HERITAGE	1
2	RUSSIA'S LITTORAL ATTACK & MIDGET SUBMARINES	11
3	DEEP SEA RESCUE VEHICLES & SUBMERSIBLES	27
4	TOURIST SUBMARINES (SUBMERSIBLES)	55
5	SUBMARINE SYSTEMS & ARMAMENT	61
6	GLOSSARY	71

INTRODUCTION

The purpose of this volume is to detail the current stable of Russian designed littoral attack submarines, midget submarines and submersibles. The evolution of small displacement Russian/Soviet submarine building is detailed, leading to the first generation Special Project 865 Piranha, Project 09070 Triton I and Project 09080 Triton II coastal and midget submarines that served the Soviet and later Russian Federation navies. The family of modern littoral submarine designs, typified by the Piranha/Piranha-T/P-550/P-650E, are detailed, as are the major submersible programs, typified by the Project 16810/16811 Rus & Project 18270 Bester deep sea rescue vehicle. The volume also covers the generation of tourist submarines designed and developed in the Soviet Union, and later the Russia Federation, from the late 1980's. The various control, sensor, communications, navigation and weapons systems that can be employed by the various submarine designs are detailed.

All technical information regarding the submarines, systems and weapons have been provided by the respective design houses, developers and builders, as has the majority of the photographic and graphic material used throughout the volume.

1

RUSSIAN/SOVIET LITTORAL SUBMARINE, MIDGET SUBMARINE & SUBMERSIBLE DESIGN HERITAGE

In October 2014, Sweden revealed that it believed its naval forces had tracked a Russian small size submarine in Swedish territorial waters (later proven to be organic debris), harking back to the 1980's when clandestine operations by Soviet (Union of Soviet Socialist Republics) and NATO (North Atlantic Treaty Organisation) underwater forces were known to have periodically taken place in Swedish waters. The Swedish accusation emerged at a time of a resurgence in small displacement coastal submarine design and development and a plethora of false (certainly lacking evidence) claims of Russian aggressive patrolling in other nations territorial waters.

In the late Cold War period of the late 1980's, the Soviet Union possessed the most capable littoral undersea warfare capability of any nation. The Soviet fleets could call on Triton-1 and Triton-2 midget Submarines and a fleet of two Special Project 865 Piranha small displacement coastal (littoral) submarines. While the Tritons were designed for coastal infiltration of combat swimmer teams, the Piranha, whilst retaining a coastal infiltration role, was intended to counter enemy warships and submarines in the Soviet Union's littoral defence zone.

Submarine design in Russia goes back to 1718, when, Efim Nikonov, working at the Admiralty yard in St Petersburg, Russia, presented a design for 'firing hidden/secret vessel' to the Tsar, Peter I (Admiralty). The vessel, which is considered to be the first manned submersible designed with armament, consisting of incendiary rockets, underwent testing at Sestroretsk after completion in 1724. The craft was submerged on three occasions, during which it suffered some damage. While this early audacious attempt at submersible craft building for military purposes has been all but forgotten, it can claim a legacy of submarine and submersible building in Russia that continues in the twenty first century. The first metal submarine in Russia was built in 1834. This craft, displacing 16.4 tons, was designed by General-Adjutant K.A. Shilder. Another submersible design with a single engine was developed in 1867, to a design drawn up by military engineer O.B. Hern.

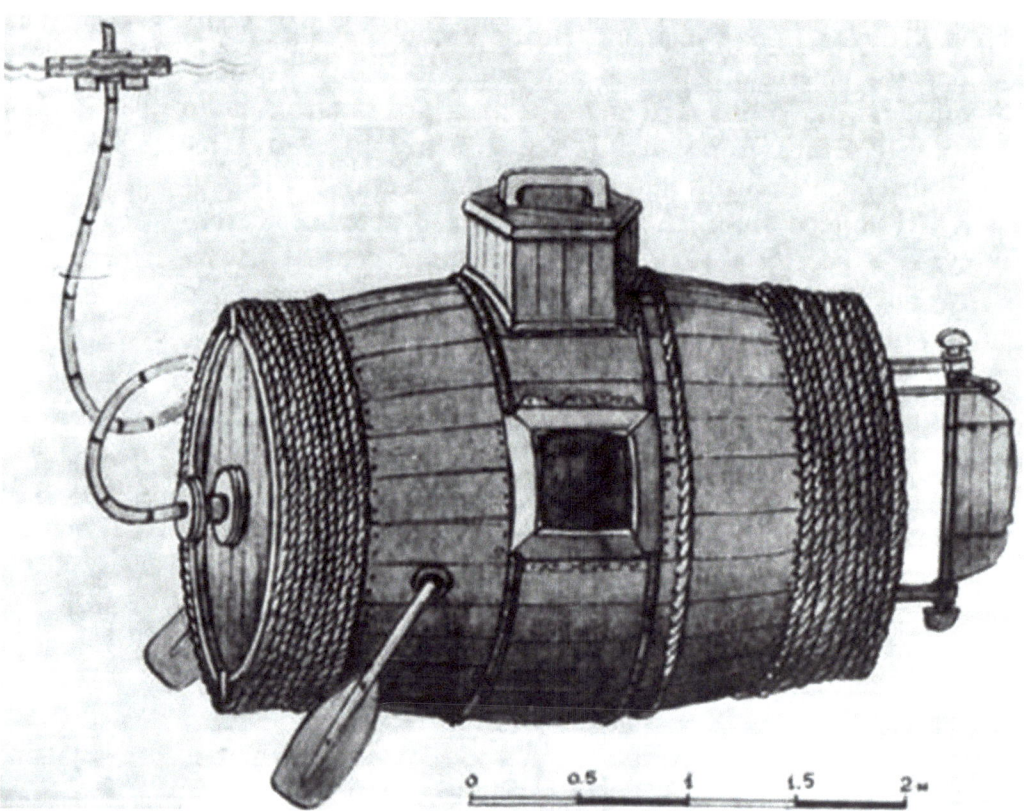

This design (replica top and rendering bottom), initiated in 1718, was presented as the first submersible in Russia designed to carry armament. The craft completed trials in 1724. Admiralty Shipyards

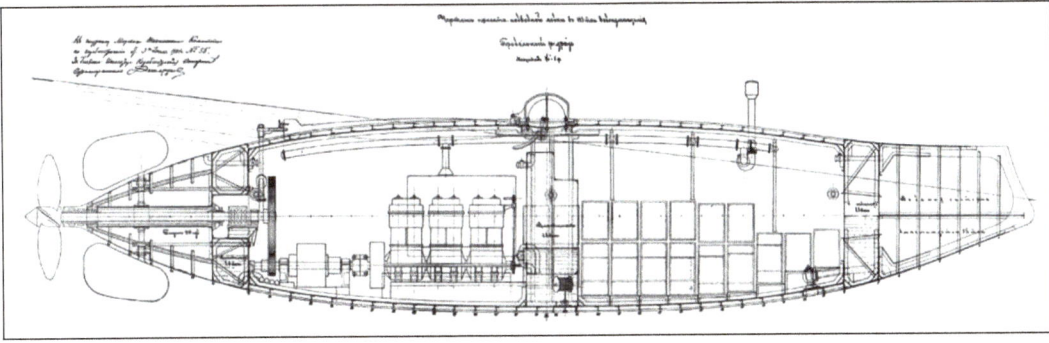

Top: The only surviving example of the SK Drzewiecki submersible, located in the Naval Museum at St Petersburg, Russia. Centre: Model of Torpedo Boat 113 (submarine) *Delphin* of 1901, the first practical Imperial Russian Navy submarine design built. Above: Design drawing of the *Delphin*. MODRF/CDB ME-Rubin

Top: The design of the first practical Russian submarine, Torpedo Boat No.113 *Delphin*, was approved in 1901 and the build and trials phase was completed in 1903. Above: The submarine *Kasatjka* was launched at the Baltic Shipyard in 1904. Six boats of this class were built for the Imperial Russian Navy. CDB ME-Rubin

The design of the first practical Russian submarine, Torpedo Boat No.113, *Delphin (Dolphin)*, was initiated in 1900, approved by the Russian Marine Ministry in 1901 and the build and trials phase was completed in 1903. The *Delphin*, as was the case with the earliest practical submarines in other countries, like the United Kingdom, were, in effect, small-size littoral submarines. In this respect, it should be considered that the modern small-size littoral submarines being marketed by the Russian Federation in the twenty first century are not design evolutions of the medium to large size submarine, but rather the medium to large size submarine designs are themselves evolutions of the small size littoral submarines of the late nineteenth and early twentieth centuries. The *Delphin* design would lead to more capable designs, the Imperial Russian Navy taking delivery of 73 submarines going into 1918, with four others undergoing construction.

The Imperial Russian Navy submarine *Lampa* (top) was laid down at the Baltic Shipyard in 1906 and construction of the submarine *Akula* (above) commenced the same year. CDB ME-Rubin

The first major submarine design of the Soviet era was the Series I, three of which were built for the Soviet Navy from 1927. In the period up to the start of the war with Germany in 1941, 206 submarines had been built to 19 different designs since the *Delphin*. A further 54 submarines were built in the Soviet Union during the war years to 1945 (CDB ME-Rubin). This included a significant number of small size submarines, commencing with the Series VI, which was designed in the period 1931-1932. This design was rail mobile so it could be transported from one theatre to another. The first of 30 units, M-1, was commissioned in 1934, these being followed by 20 of the Series VI-bis. Design of the Series XII small size submarine commenced in 1936, the first of 46 units of this class, M-171, being commissioned into the Soviet Navy in 1937. Another small size submarine was the Series XV, the first of 57 units of this class, M-200, being commissioned into the Soviet Navy in 1943. The Design 95, initiated in 1939, was a small size experimental submarine utilising a closed cycle with chemical line absorber power system when submerged. The single vessel of this class, M-401, commissioned into the Soviet Navy in 1946. The Project 615 small experimental submarine, M-254, was designed from 1948 to test a closed cycle propulsion system – single engine. Trials of this vessel, which was commissioned in 1953, demonstrated a submerged speed of 15 knots. The Project 615 evolved into the Project A615 class, which numbered 30 boats.

Legacy deep water submersibles include the North-2 autonomous inhabited self-propelled submersible, built at Admiralty shipyards in 1970. This design, which was capable of submerging to a depth of 2000 m, was used to explore flora in many areas of the world's oceans, including the Ross Sea in Antarctica. A family of 'towed underwater chambers' was built at Admiralty Shipyards in 1972. Two Atlant-2 (diving depth, 300 m); six Project 1605 Tethys and four Project 1605I Tetis-N (Admiralty). These units were used for a number of oceanic survey missions, including the World War I and World War II chemical weapon dumping sites (Admiralty). The Project 1602 Tinro-2 'self-propelled double underwater vehicle' of 1973 was capable of submerging to a depth of 400 m (Admiralty). The Tinro-2 was involved in underwater research in the Bering, Black and Okhotsk seas, areas off the coast of the continent of Africa, the Bermuda Triangle region and, in 1993, the complex was employed in the operation to recover wreckage from the Korean Air Lines Boeing 747 Flight 007 – shot down by Soviet interceptors in 1983 – in the sea of the coast of Sakhalin Island in the Russian Federation Far East (Admiralty). The Project 1832 Piosk-2 of 1975, described as an 'autonomous habitable self-propelled experimental device', was capable of submerging to depths of 2000 m (Admiralty). The Project 1905 Piosk-6 'self-contained deep-water submersible' was designed in 1983 and entered service in August 1985 – this complex was able to explore the extreme depths of the Kuril Ridge in the Pacific Ocean, down to a depth of 6015 m (Admiralty).

Previous page top: Project A615 small-size submarine. Previous page bottom: The North-2 autonomous inhabited self-propelled submersible, built at Admiralty shipyards in 1970, was capable of submerging to a depth of 2000 m. Above: Project 16051 Tetis-N towed underwater vehicle of 1972. CDB ME-Rubin/Admiralty

Previous page top: The Project 1602 Tinro-2 self-propelled double underwater vehicle of 1973 was capable of submerging to a depth of 400 m. Previous page bottom: The Project 1832 Piosk-2 of 1975 was capable of submerging to a depth of 2000 m. This page top: The Project 1905 Piosk-6 was designed in 1983 and entered service in August 1985 – this complex was able to explore the Kuril Ridge in the Pacific Ocean, down to a depth of 6015 m. Above: Project 940 Lenok (allocated the NATO reporting name 'India') submersible carrier submarine. Admiralty Shipyards/US DoD

Top: The Project 940 Lenok was a two boat class designed to accommodate two submersibles, such as the Project 18551 deep sea rescue vehicle. These were housed in upper deck wells and could be launched for underwater rescue operations when the Lenok mothership was submerged. This page top: The MKT-200 tracked marine complex was in service with the Soviet naval forces in the 1980's. The vehicles role was stated by the Ministry of Defence of the Russian Federation as to facilitate underwater surveys of objects, such as a sunken submarine. The complex could attach an air pipe to a sunken submarine to assist the crew awaiting rescue, and could assist in repairing a vessels hull. The MK-200 may well be a culprit in the alleged Soviet covert underwater operations in Swedish territorial waters, if, indeed, such operations actually took place. US DoD/Lazurit/MODRF

2

RUSSIA'S LITTORAL ATTACK & MIDGET SUBMARINES

In the late Cold War period of the mid to late 1980's, western media was enthralled with tales, much of which was fantasy, of small size Soviet submarine and submersible operations in the coastal waters of NATO (North Atlantic Treaty Organisation) nations and non-aligned nations, particularly Sweden – the Baltic Sea and Gulf of Finland were particular hotbeds of activity, actual and imagined. In the 1970's and 1980's, the Soviet Union developed and deployed a number of small size coastal and midget submarines, most notably the Special Project 865 Piranha (allocated the NATO reporting name Losos) coastal submarine and the Project 09070 Triton-1 and Project 09080 Triton-2 midget submarines, this having no little impact on the suspicions of undersea skullduggery.

The perception of western observers as to the assumed shenanigans of the Soviet Union in NATO and non-aligned nations coastal waters was fueled by the emergence of the Project 940 Lenok (allocated the NATO reporting name 'India'), which was designed to carry two DSRV (Deep Sea Rescue Vehicles) to provide a measure of rescue capability for disabled submerged or sunken submarines. It was speculated. Again no supporting evidence emerging, that an alternative purpose for these submarines was the transportation of midget submarines, from which Soviet combat swimmers would operate on sabotage and reconnaissance operations. The 'India' class boats were decommissioned in the early to mid-1990s.

Although the two Special Project 865 submarines and a number of the Triton-1/2 are still nominally on the strength of the Russian Federation Navy, they are, as far as can be ascertained, in reserve, with no allocated operational tasking. It is unclear if the Russian Federation Navy will acquire modern small submarines in the mold of the Triton-1/2 or Piranha vessels. However, the resurgence of small submarine development in Russia has resulted in renewed claims of Russian aggressive patrolling in other nations territorial waters, nothing in the way of actual evidence so far having been presented by NATO or other parties such as Sweden. The claim by Sweden that it tracked a Russian small size submarine in Swedish territorial waters in October 2014 lacked credibility through lack of evidence. With no visual identification the object could have been any of a number of things ranging from equipment blips, submerged debris, wildlife, or, on a less serious note, Scotland's own Nessie on vacation in Swedish waters. While it was eventually confirmed that the object was not a Russian submarine, but rather, organic debris, the incident fueled the confrontational elements of the political machinations as NATO and the EU (European Union) embarked upon a campaign to portray Russia as the bogyman of Europe following Crimea's 2014 democratic decision, through public referendum, to reunify with the Russian Federation in the wake of the western supported coup in Ukraine. This was followed by a continual stream of scaremongering by western political and senior military figures about what Russia could do to cause disruption to western countries on the world's oceans – for example, cut communications lines (including internet) leaving the NATO alliance reliant on vulnerable satellite communications. In 2019, a Russian naval vessel can barely put to sea without a western media frenzy about a potential threat to NATO, despite there being no uninvited incursions into other nation's territorial waters. While this may be deviating from the subject matter of the volume, it serves to highlight the fact that unsubstantiated media reports can be used as a political tool to present fiction as fact – in this case Russia was accused of operating submersibles in foreign waters when there was absolutely no evidence to support the claim or, indeed, that any of the Special Project 865 submarines are employed in anything other than a technology development support role.

In the second decade of the twenty first century, the Triton 1/2 and Piranha type vessels are still being promoted. In addition, there are a number of more modern designs, ranging from the Piranha-T to the P-550 and P-650E small submarines, all designed by Malachite SPB JSC – these designs are primarily aimed at the export market.

Top: One of the two Special Project 865 Piranha small coastal submarines built for the Soviet Navy in the 1980's. USC

One of the two Piranha boats in dockyard hands. The partially complete outer hull reveals the double hull design of this class of vessel.

Special Project 865 Piranha small littoral submarine – In the mid-1970's, the Soviet Union began to field a fleet of midget submarines of the Triton-1 and Triton-2 types for special forces operations; these being joined in the mid-1980's by the larger Special Project 865 Piranha small submarines for coastal and special forces operations. Described as a small coastal submarine, vessels of the Piranha class are designed to attack surface and sub-surface vessels with torpedoes, conduct mine laying and reconnaissance in littoral waters and further afield, as well as insertion and extraction of raiding forces of combat swimmers. The Piranha vessels, which were specifically designed for operations in shallow water, inaccessible to larger diesel electric and nuclear powered attack submarines, proved to be very difficult to detect due to their titanium alloy construction, the poor magnetism nature of the structure making them all but immune to modern sensors such as MAD (Magnetic Anomaly Detection).

Developed under the design leadership of L.V. Chernopyatov, two Special Project 865 boats, MS-520 and MS-521, were built at Admiralty Shipyard in Leningrad, USSR (Union of Soviet Socialist Republics) – now St. Petersburg, Russian – the first of these being laid down in 1984, launched in 1986 and commissioned in 1988. The second boat entered service in 1990. In 2019, both of these vessels are thought to be non–operational, held in reserve, with one, as noted above, possibly employed to test technologies for the new generation small size submarines marketed in Russia.

There are two design specifications issued by the builder for the Piranha, these being option 1 and option 2. It is unclear if the two boats were built one to each specification or if the option 2 specification was unbuilt. Option 1 was constructed of titanium alloy, option 2 would replace titanium with steel.

The Piranha of 1984 could deploy a team of combat swimmers on the surface or at depths down to 60 m (Admiralty), complementing the Triton dedicated combat swimmer deployment vehicles.

One of the two Special Project 865 Piranha small coastal submarines built for the Soviet Navy and inherited by what would become the Russian Federation Navy when the Soviet Union was dissolved in December 1991. Malachite

Technical specification, Special Project 865 Piranha option 1 – data furnished by USC/Admiralty Shipyards/Malachite SPB

Housing material: Titanium alloy
Main propulsion plant: diesel electric, 1 x 160 kW diesel generator and 1 x 60 kW direct propulsion current motor
Normal displacement: 220 m^3 (USC value) or 218 m^3 (Admiralty Shipyards value)
Length: 30 m (USC value) or 28.2 m (Admiralty Shipyards value)
Beam: 4.7 m
Draught (draft): 3.9 m
Maximum diving depth: 200 m
Full underwater speed: 6.6 knots
Economic underwater speed: 4.0 knots
Surface speed: ~8 knots
Cruising speed: 4 knots
Cruising range at cruising speed: 1,000 nm
Continuous submerged range (electrochemical generator): 260 nm (USC value) or 130 miles (Admiralty Shipyards value)
Endurance: 10 days
Complement: 3 crew with accommodation provided for 6 combat swimmers
Armament: 2 x 324 mm (400 mm class) Latush torpedoes or 533 mm class mines
Watertight pressure containers for equipment for combat swimmers: 2

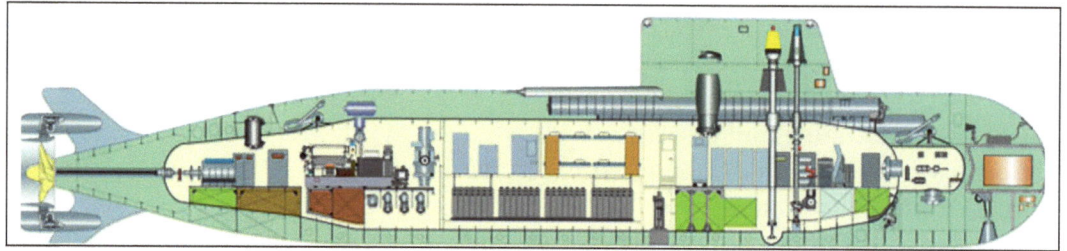

Previous page: A Special Project 865 Piranha small size submarine. Above: Special Project 865 Piranha Option 2 cutaway diagram. Malachite

The two boats of the Piranha class of small littoral submarines combined the combat swimmer insertion mission with a coastal attack submarine role. These boats were the forerunners of Piranha-T, P-550 and P-650E littoral submarines designs. USC

Technical specification, Special Project 865 Piranha Option 2 – data furnished by USC/Admiralty Shipyards

Housing material: Steel
Main propulsion plant: diesel electric, 1 x 315 kW diesel generator and 220 kW propulsion current motor
Normal displacement: 330 m³
Length: 38.2 m
Beam: 4.3 m
Draught: 3.9 m
Maximum diving depth: 200 m
Full underwater speed: 6.6 knots (USC value). Admiralty states a full underwater speed of 10 knots and an economic underwater speed 4 knots
Surface speed: ~8 knots
Cruising speed: 4 knots
Cruising range at cruising speed: 1,130 nm
Continuous submerged range (electrochemical generator): 120 miles
Endurance: 10 days
Complement: 5 crew with accommodation provided for 6 combat swimmers
Armament: 2 x 324 mm Latush torpedoes or 533 mm mines
Watertight pressure containers for equipment for combat swimmers: 2

The improved Piranha-T, as was the case with the P-550 and P-650E, was designed under the leadership of J.K. Mineev. The Piranha-T, like the Piranha, would be powered by a diesel generator and battery storage propulsion system. Projected performance was increased, as was armament capability. This appears to be at the expense of removal of the facility for carrying a combat swimmer team, according to United Shipbuilding Corporation documentation. Contradicting this, Admiralty Shipyards documentation shows the retention of accommodation for the six combat swimmers, although watertight pressure containers for combat swimmer equipment appears to have been omitted. The Piranha-T can accommodate 2 x Sirena-UM swimmer delivery vehicles, although this would be at the expense of the torpedo armament.

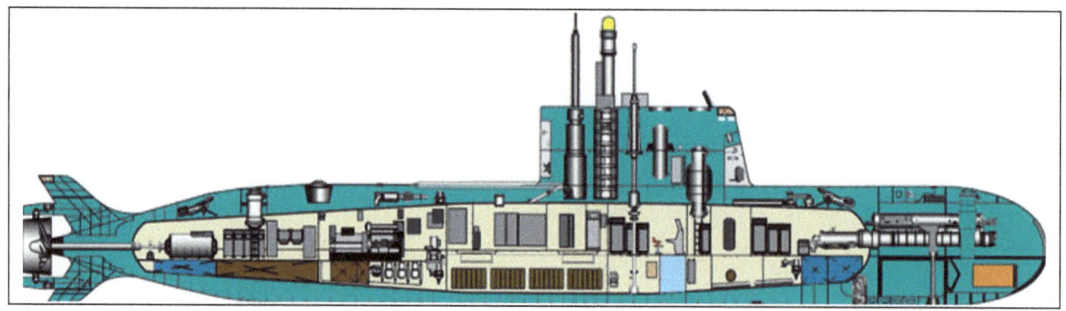

Previous page: Three quarters frontal aspect view (top) and a port side aspect view (bottom) of design modelling of the **Piranha-T** small size coastal submarine. Above: Cutaway diagram of the **Piranha-T** small coastal submarine. Malachite

> Technical specification, Piranha-T – data furnished by USC/Admiralty Shipyards
>
> **Main propulsion plant:** diesel electric, 1 x 315 kW diesel generator and 400 kW propulsion motor
> **Normal displacement:** 245 m^3 (USC value) or 370 m^3 (Admiralty Shipyards value)
> **Length:** 30 m (USC value) or 47.5 m (Admiralty Shipyards value)
> **Beam:** 4.7 m (USC value) or 5.2 m (Admiralty Shipyards value)
> **Draught (draft):** 3.9 m
> **Maximum diving depth:** 200 m
> **Full underwater speed:** 12 knots
> **Cruising speed:** 4 knots
> **Cruising range at cruising speed:** 2,000 nm (USC value) or 2,200 miles (Admiralty Shipyards value)
> **Continuous submerged range (electrochemical generator):** 260 nm (USC value) or 200 miles (Admiralty Shipyards value)
> **Endurance:** 20 days
> **Complement:** 5 crew plus provision for 6 combat swimmers
> **Armament:** 8 x 324 mm (400 mm class) torpedoes, 2 x 533 mm class torpedoes and 4 mines (USC values) or 6 x 324 mm torpedo and 2 x 533 mm torpedo/missile (Club-S) or, alternatively, 8 mines (Admiralty Shipyards values)

The Piranha-2 was marketed through the first decade of the twenty first century, but this variant, which would have had a displacement of around 400 m^3, a length of 31 m, beam 5.8 m and a draught of 5.4 m, appears to have been dropped as United Shipbuilding Corporation concentrated on promoting an updated Piranha designated Piranha-T. This was in line with concentration on the P-550 and P-650E small coastal submarines, which emerged from a plethora of such designs being promoted in the first decade of the twenty first century. The P-550/650E classes were considerably larger than the Piranha-T.

Top: Port side view of design modelling of the P-550 small coastal submarine. Above: Starboard side-on view design modelling of the P-550 small size littoral submarine. Malachite

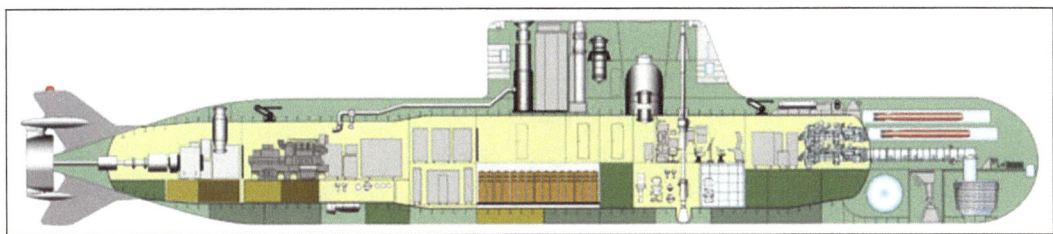

P-550 small coastal submarine cutaway diagram. Malachite

Project P-550 small coastal submarine – The Project P-550 class of small submarine was designed to patrol shallow coastal waters and to be capable of engaging surface warships and submarines with torpedoes, laying minefields and attacking fixed coastal targets with 3M-14E land attack cruise missiles. Other roles would include the insertion and extraction of combat swimmers and conducting reconnaissance against enemy coastal areas.

Technical Specification, P-550 small coastal submarine – data furnished by USC/Admiralty Shipyards/Malachite SPB

Main propulsion plant: Diesel electric and storage battery – 1 x 630 kW or 2 x 350 kW diesel generator and 900 kW propulsion motor
Normal displacement: 650 m^3 (USC value) or 750 m^3 (Admiralty Shipyards & Malachite SPB value)
Length: 51 m (USC value) or 55.1 m (Admiralty Shipyards & Malachite SPB value)
Beam: 6.4 m
Draught (draft): 4.9 m
Maximum operating depth: 300 m
Full underwater speed: 15.5 knots (USC value) or 14.5 knots (Admiralty value)
Cruising speed: 4 knots
Cruising range at cruising speed: 2,000 nm (USC value) or 2,200 miles (Admiralty Shipyards value)
Continuous submerged range: 200 nm (USC value) or 160 miles (Admiralty value)
Endurance: 20 days
Complement: 9 crew with accommodation for a 6 person combat swimmer team
Armament: 8 x 400 mm class (324 mm) torpedoes and 4 x 533 mm torpedoes/Club-S cruise missiles and 12 mines or, alternatively, a maximum of 24 mines

Project P-650E small coastal submarine – The project P-650E is an evolution of the Project P-550, having the same beam, but with an increased length and higher displacement, both being designed for the same mission. The P-650E is more capable in a number of respects, not least of which is the vastly increased continuous submerged endurance, courtesy of the addition of AIP (Air Independent Propulsion) to the standard diesel-electric propulsion suite.

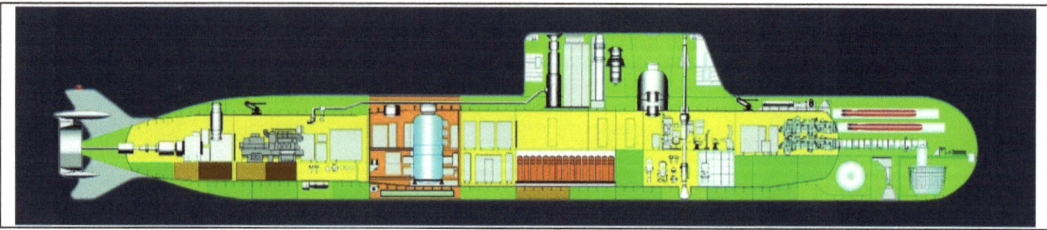

Top: P-650E small coastal submarine cutaway diagram. USC

Above: Starboard (ghosted) and port side-on views of the P-650E. Malachite

Technical Specification, P-650E small coastal submarine – data furnished by USC/Admiralty Shipyards

Main propulsion plant: Diesel electric and storage battery – 1 x 630 kW diesel generator and 900 kW propulsion motor, with provision for Air Independent Propulsion with 15000 kWh electrochemical oxygen-hydrogen generators plus storage battery – this considerably increases the time the boat can stay submerged
Normal displacement: 760 m^3 (USC value) or 870 m^3 (Admiralty Shipyard value)
Length: 57 m (USC value) or 60.5 m (Admiralty Shipyard value)
Beam: 6.4 m
Draught (draft): 5 m
Maximum operating depth: 300 m
Full underwater speed: 15 knots (USC value) or 14 knots (Admiralty value)
Cruising speed: 4 knots
Cruising range at cruising speed: 2,000 nm
Continuous submerged range (electrochemical generator): 1,200 nm
Endurance: 20 days
Complement: 9 crew with accommodation for a 6 person combat swimmer team
Armament: 8 x 324 mm (400 mm class) torpedoes and 4 x 533 mm torpedoes/Club-S cruise missiles and 12 mines or, alternatively, up to 24 mines

Although not actively promoted in 2019, over the previous decade or so there has been a number of additional small size submarines offered from Russian submarine builders. These include the P-650B, which was basically a P-650E with a diesel generator plus closed cycle diesel power plant. The P-750, with a length of 62 m, bean 6.4 m, draught 7.3 m and displacement 860 m^3, the P-750B, with a length of 68 m, beam 6.4 m, draught 7.3 m, displacement 920 m^3 and P-750E, with a length of 69.5 m, beam 6.4 m, draught 7.3 m and displacement 920 m^3, were basically enlarged versions of the P-550, P-650B and P-650E respectively. Their larger size would have allowed for the accommodation of four 3M-54E land attack cruise missiles housed in standard containers. At the smaller end of the scale was the P-130 and P-170, the former having a length of 31 m, beam 3 m, draught 5.2 m, a displacement of 130 m^3 and the latter having a length of 30 m, beam 4 m, draught 5.1 m and a displacement of 170 m^3. These designs would have had similar performance parameters and endurance to the Piranha-T, being powered by the same diesel generator and storage battery system (Rosoboronexport).

Project 09070 Triton-1 & Project 09080 Triton-2 Midget Submarines – The Triton-1 and Triton-2 are a family of midget submarines designed, not for a combat role in that they would engage targets such as surface ships, but as the transport system for small size combat swimmer teams tasked with planting mines or conducting reconnaissance of enemy controlled coastal areas and ports. The vessels, which are constructed from anti-corrosive materials, are equipped with a suite of navigation and communications equipment and a stationary air regeneration system. The vessels would normally be transported to a drop of point by a mothership, either a surface craft or a submarine.

Both the Tritpn-1 and the larger Triton-2, which were developed in the early 1970's under the design leadership of Y.E. Evgrafov, were built at Admiralty shipyards in Leningrad (now St. Petersburg). The first Triton-1 was made operable in 1973 and the first Triton-2 was made ready in 1974. In total 32 Triton-1/M and 13 of the larger Triton-2 craft were built (Admiralty Shipyards).

Starboard side-on view graphics of a Project 09070 Triton-1 two-person midget submarine. Malachite

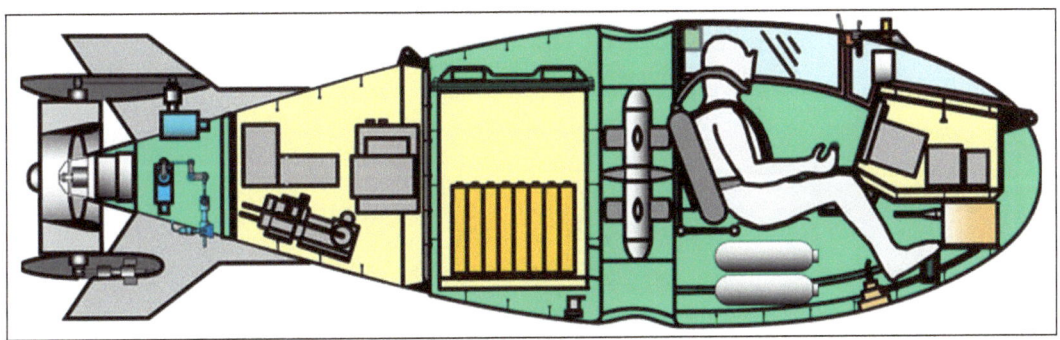

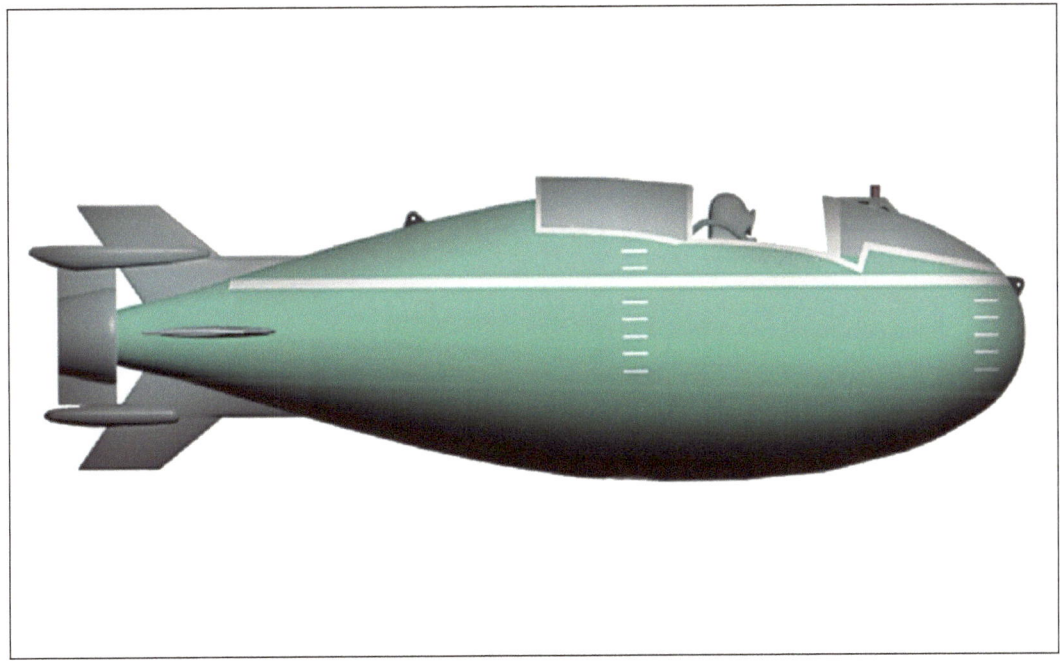

Top: Port side-on view graphic of a Project 09070 Triton-1 two-person midget submarine. **Centre:** Project 09070 Triton-1 cutaway graphic. **Above:** Project 09070 Triton-1 starboard profile. Malachite/USC

Technical Specification, Triton 1 midget submarine – data furnished by USC/Malachite SPB

Developer: Malachite Design Bureau/33 Shipyard
Hull material: aluminium-magnesium alloy
Normal displacement on surface: 1.6 m^3
Length: ~5 m
Beam of hull: 1.4 m
Height of hull: 1.4 m
Reserve buoyancy: about 8% to the normal displacement
Maximum operating depth: 40 m
Full underwater speed: ~6 knots
Cruising underwater range at 6 knots speed: 35 nm
Endurance: around 6 hours
Complement: 2 person Mr. Rupp combat swimmer team

Starboard (top) and port (above) side-on digital model graphics of a six-person Project 09080 Triton-2 midget submarine. Malachite

Technical Specification, Triton 2 midget submarine – data furnished by USC/Malachite SPB, with additional input from Rosoboronexport

Developer: Malachite Design Bureau/33 Shipyard
Hull material: aluminium-magnesium alloy
Normal displacement: 4.4 m^3
Length: about 9 m (USC value) or 9.5 m Rosoboronexport value)
Beam of hull: 1.6 m (USC value) or 2.0 m Rosoboronexport value)
Height of hull: 1.6 m (USC value) or 2.2 m (Rosoboronexport value)
Reserve buoyancy: about 8% to the normal displacement
Maximum operating depth: 40 m
Full underwater speed: about 6 knots
Buoyancy, as a percentage of the normal displacement: 8
Underwater cruising range at 6 knots speed: 60 nm
Endurance: around 12 hours
Complement: 6 person combat swimmer team

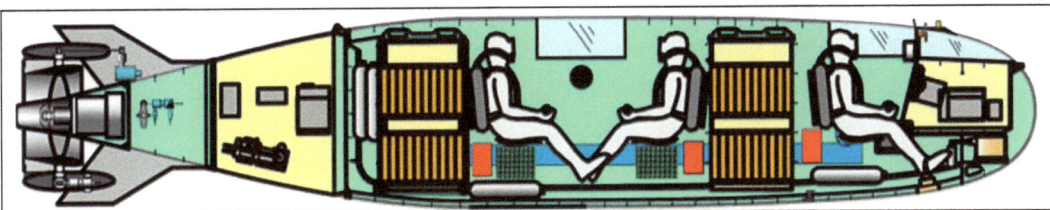

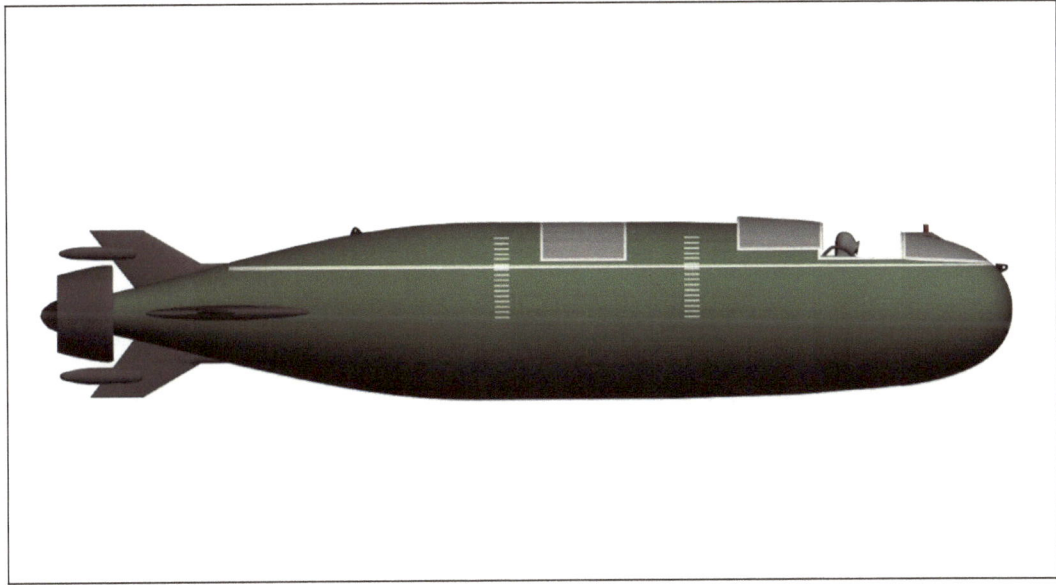

Top: **Project 09080 Triton-2 midget submarine ghosted graphic.** Above: **Project 09080 Triton-2 midget submarine profile layout.** Malachite

Special Project 865 Piranha				
S/N	Shipyard	Laid Down	Launched	Commissioned
MS-520	Admiralty	1984	1986	1988
MS-521	Admiralty	c.1986	c-1988	1990

Triton 1 – 32 built for Soviet Navy
Triton 2 – 13 built for Soviet Navy

Note: Both Special Project 865 Piranha vessels are apparently held in reserve, although one or more may be used in a trials capacity to test systems for the new generation of small size submarine designs

Top: A Project 09080 Triton-2 midget submarine. Above: Graphics depicting the Poseidon deep ocean nuclear strike small submersible exiting the storage bay of its nuclear powered submarine carrier. As such platforms are designed for a strategic strike role they are outside the remit of this volume. MODRF

3

DEEP SEA RESCUE VEHICLES & SUBMERSIBLES

The Russian Federation currently operates two types of DSRV (Deep Sea Rescue Vehicle) – the Project 18551, designed in the Soviet era, and the Project 18270 Bester, which entered service in the second decade of the twenty first century. In addition, several deep sea inhabited submersible designs are operated for a number of specialised roles, including assist of underwater rescue and salvage operations, within the Russian naval fleets and the civil sector.

Project 16810 and Project 16811 Standalone Rus Deep Diving Submersible – Having previously produced a number of deep sea submersible vehicles, including the Mir-1 and Mir-2 vehicles, the Soviet Union, and later the Russian Federation, continued development of such vehicles for rescue work, research, exploration and engineering work. The Project 16810 and Project 16811 designs are deep diving submersibles that can operate at depths down to 6000 m. The vessels are designed to perform technical tasks and assist in sub-surface rescue operations. Another task is the detection of and installation of tracking beacons on underwater objects. An onboard camera suite can be used to perform inspections of underwater locations and vessels or platforms in distress, such as a disabled submarine on the sea floor. The vehicles can capture sub surface objects weighing up to 200 kg and carry then to the sea surface. For this role the submersibles are equipped with an SKM-1 manipulator complex, which incorporates 'two executive bodies, a control panel' and steering equipment (Admiralty). The SKM-1 manipulator complex can be used to lift or move objects that may be obstructing a submarine escape hatch to allow for docking of deep sea rescue vehicle, transported and operated from a surface mothership (USC & Admiralty).

Although the Project 16810/16811 vehicles are designed to be capable of assisting submerged submarines in distress, their main mission is site survey and repair work in the civil industries. This includes survey/repair of oil and gas pipes and other sub-surface facilities, as well as sub-surface archeology and camera work (USC & Admiralty).

Project 16810 (top) and Project 16811 (above) standalone Rus deep diving submersibles. Admiralty Shipyards

Page 29 top: Project 16810. Page 29 bottom and page 30: The Project 16811 Standalone Rus deep diving submersible is clearly an evolution of the Project 16810 vehicle, both having the same overall dimensions and performance characteristics.
Malachite

Page 31-33: Project 16811. Admiralty Shipyards/Malachite

Technical Specification, Project 16810 – data furnished by USC/Admiralty Shipyards
Housing length, maximum: 8.4 m
Housing width, maximum: 3.9 m
Housing height, maximum: 3.85 m
Weight, sludge, buoyancy
Weight, prepared by the descent of the AHA: about 25 tons
Cake (average) from the bottom edge of the supports: 2.6 m
Fence rook elevation above the waterline: about 1 m
Reserve buoyancy: 1.8 m^3
Operating depth: down to 6000 m
Horizontal maximum submerged speed: 2.6 knots
Dive time to maximum depth under certain conditions: around 3 hours
Ascent time from maximum depth under certain conditions: around 3 hours
Working endurance: 12 hours
Maximum emergency endurance: 72 hours
Crew: 2 normal with provision for a third if required

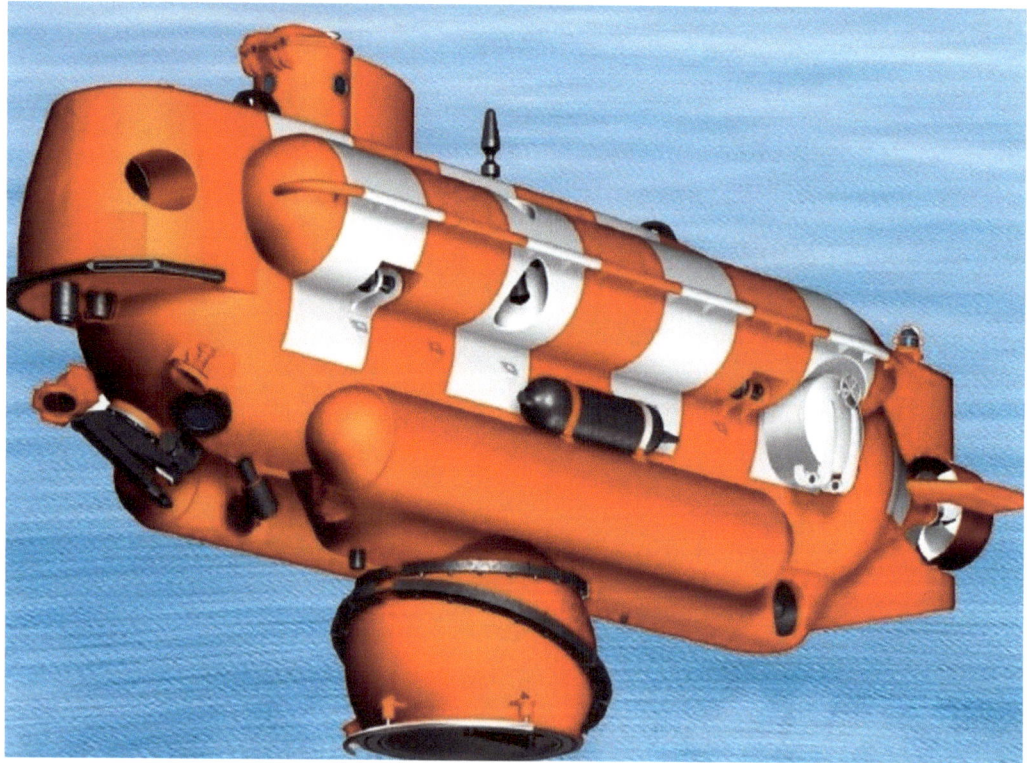

Top: Project 18270 Bester deep sea rescue vehicle. **Above:** External layout of the **Project 18270 Bester** Admiralty/Rosoboronexport

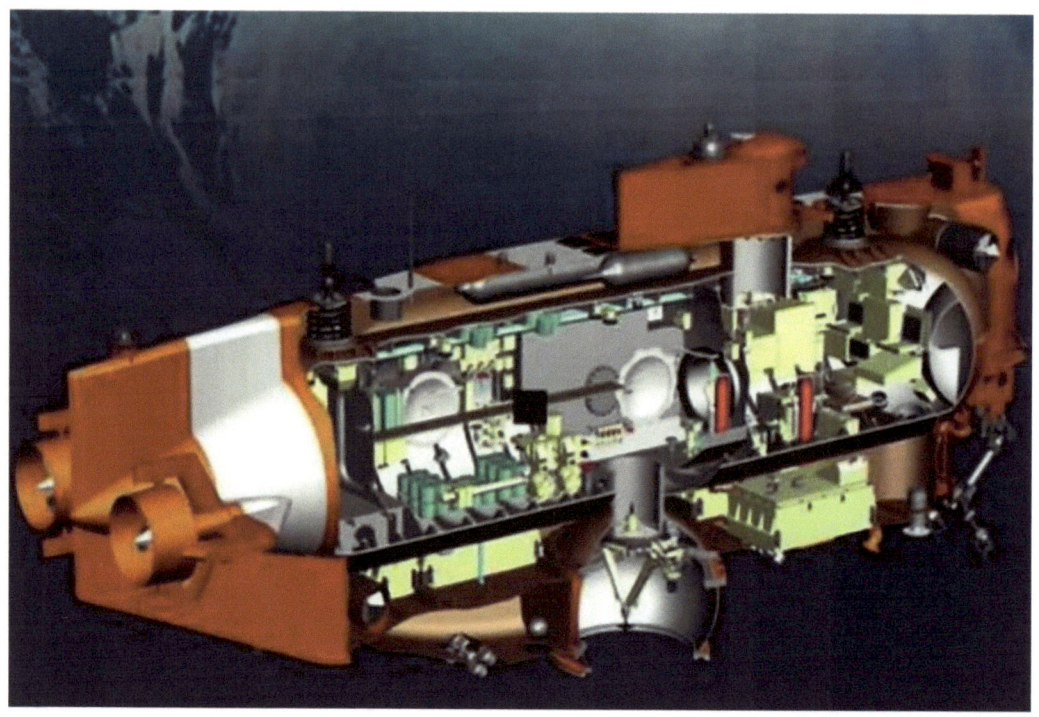

Previous page: Port side-on graphic (top) and three-quarters rear-on graphic (bottom) of the Project 18270 Bester deep sea rescue vehicle. Above: Cutaway graphic showing the internal layout of the Project 18270 Bester. CDB Lazurit

Project 18270 Bester deep sea rescue vehicle – The Project 18270 Bester (also referred to as the Bestor-1 (domestic) and Bester-E (export standard), described as a fourth generation SGA (Admiralty), was designed in co-operation by CDB ME-Rubin and CDB-Lazurit. Bester builds on the capabilities of previous generation rescue submersibles, such as the Project 1937, 1837, 18551, 19551, LR5 and Nemo submersibles.

The Bester submersible can be employed in rescue operations of submerged submarines in distress as well as other underwater platforms. The craft, which operates from a Project 21301 Rescue and Salvage Vessel, can be docked with other craft at up to a 45° sloping surface. This is a significant advance on the capabilities of previous generation deep sea rescue submersibles, which were limited to roll angles of around 15° (Admiralty). Rescue operations can be conducted at depths down to around 800 m (CDB-Lazurit states 790 m). The vehicle can carry 18 rescued persons (Admiralty Shipyards states 22 rescued persons) to the surface per trip, or, alternatively, can be used to raise objects with a weight up to 1.5 tones (CDB ME-Rubin & Admiralty). The life support systems for crew and rescued personnel can operate at various pressure settings in the recue compartment. The system is capable of operating in a dry and wet environment. A flow pressurization system allows the commencement of decompression of rescued personnel during the ascent phase of the operation, thus reducing the time required in the decompression chambers aboard the Project 21301 Rescue and Salvage Vessel (Admiralty).

Bester can be transported by sea, rail or air, allowing the submersibles to be moved from one theatre to another. Three of the Project 21301 Salvage and Rescue Vessels were ordered, one for each of the Russian Federation Northern, Pacific and Baltic fleets. The lead Project 21301 vessel, *Igor Belousov*, which was laid down on 24 December 2005, was delivered to her Pacific Fleet home port of Vladivostok in summer 2016 (Almaz).

While rescue of crews of sunken or distressed submarines is the Besters primary mission the craft can also be employed for other purposes, such as conducing technical works at various depths and inspecting underwater material/infrastructure (Admiralty).

Project 18270 Bester deep sea rescue vehicle. Admiralty Shipyards

Technical Specification, Project 18270 – data furnished by CDB ME-Rubin/CDB Lazurit/Admiralty Shipyards/Rosoboronexport

Hull material: titanium alloy
Normal displacement: 39 m^3 (Rosoboronexport states about 36 m^3 normal and 39 m^3 full load), Admiralty shipyards states about 41 tons
Length: about 12 m (CDB ME-Rubin value) or 11.9 m (CDB Lazurit/Admiralty Shipyards value)
Beam: 3.2 m
Height: 5 m (CDB ME-Rubin value) or 5.2 m (CDB Lazurit/Admiralty Shipyards value)
Maximum operating depth: 800 m (CDB ME-Rubin value) or 790 m (CDB Lazurit/Admiralty Shipyards value)
Life support endurance: 72 hours for crew only and 10 hours for crew and rescued personnel
Maximum submerged speed, horizontal (ahead and astern): 3.2 knots
Maximum submerged speed, vertical: 0.65 knots
Maximum submerged speed, lateral (sideways): 0.45 knots
Range: 9 nm
Battery capacity: 400 A x hour
Complement: 3 crew with accommodation for 18 rescued persons (Admiralty Shipyards documentation states 3 crew and 22 rescued persons)
Permissible pressure in the rescue compartment: 0.6 MPa
Endurance: about 12 hours

Project 18270 Bester deep sea rescue vehicle. Admiralty Shipyards

Project 21301 Salvage and Rescue Vessel – The major mothership platform for the Project 18270 Bester is the Project 21301 Salvage and Rescue Vessel, the first of which entered service in 2016. It is unfortunate that certain elements of mainstream western media, with their enormous reach, perpetuate the misinformation as to the Project 21301 role – spy ships rather than rescue and salvage vessels. The reasons for this are open to speculation – possibly for disinformation purposes to aid in achieving a political aim or possibly through a simple lack of understanding of the vessels true function. Whatever the reasoning behind this disservice, it makes it difficult for the non-biased researcher, whom goes with the facts as the most logical hypothesis based on the best available data. In the United Kingdom, the national broadcaster has produced misleading material that perpetuates the spy ship misinformation as fact. As this was accomplished in similar timeframes that had senior military officials being rolled out to warn about the Russian threat and a general anti-Russian hysteria throughout much of the British political and media establishments, one could not be faulted for forming the hypothesis that the spy ship claim is intended to show Russia as a malign force in the world. To assume the vessels are spy ships based on their being equipped with detections sensors, required to locate stricken vessels, would effectively place any oceanographic research vessel or, indeed, a wide range of commercial vessel in the spy ship category.

Page 39-40: Project 21301 salvage and rescue ship. Admiralty/MODRF

The Project 21301 vessels are outfitted to operate Bester submersibles and are equipped with a sophisticated sensor suite for the detection of a disabled submarine on the sea floor or maintaining buoyancy, but unable to surface. If required, other submersibles, such as the Rus projects, can be carried. A suite of equipment and rescue systems provisions for assisting or rescuing crews of submarines or surface vessels. This includes the ability to support diving operations and provide technical work teams for underwater repair or assessment of damage. As well as the inhabited submersibles, the Project 21301 can also operate uninhabited submersibles or ROV (Remotely Operated Vehicles) (Almaz & Admiralty).

The Project 21301 ships are powered by 4 x 2100 kW diesel-generators with 2 x 1680 kW auxiliary diesel-generators and a single 1080 kW harbor diesel-generator. Electrical Power is provided through a JEPS (Joint Electrical Power System), consisting of two propelling electric motors that drive the 3600 kW, 360° rudder-propellers, a pair of 850 kW thrusters and two main switchboards, all controlled through a JEWS distribution and control system (Almaz).

As well as the Bester DSRV, which can operate down to depths of 300 m, and a single ROV that can operate down to depths of 1000 m, the Project 21301 feature an extensive mission associated equipment fit. As well as the deep water diving suite that provides for the saturation diving rescue operations to depths of 300 m, a diving bell is provided with accommodation for up to three persons. Rescued personnel can be accommodated in four habitable decompression chambers once brought aboard. Boats available for rescue operations consist of a duty boat and a hyperbaric rescue boat. 12.5 ft. hydraulic cranes are provided for the lifting of submersibles to and from the water. A flight deck for helicopter operations is provided on the forward section of the ship, but no hanger facilities are provided for permanent helicopter basing.

Technical specification, Project 21301 – data furnished by Almaz Central Marine Design Bureau

Standard displacement: 5800 tons
Dimensions: ~117 x 18.3 m
Speed: 17 knots
Endurance: 45 days for crew and 10 days with rescues brought aboard
Range: 5,000 nm
Crew: 97
Machinery: 4 x 2100 kW diesel-generators, 2 x 1680 kW auxiliary diesel-generators and 1 x 1080 kW harbor diesel-generator
JEPS (Joint Electrical Power System): 2 x propelling electric motors, each driving a 3500 kW 360° rudder propeller; 2 x 850 kW thrusters; 2 main switchboards and a JEPS distribution and control system
RESCUE EQUIPMENT
1 x deep submergence rescue vehicle capable of operating down to depths of 300 m
1 x work and recue launch with a capacity for twelve persons
1 x duty boat
1 x deep water diving suite for saturation diving operations down to depths of 300 m
4 x habitable decompression chambers
1 x diving bell with accommodation for three persons
1 x hyperbaric lifeboat
2 x 12.5 ft. capable electric hydraulic cranes
1 x remotely operated vehicle, operating down to depths of 1000 m
1 x equipment set for the non-permanent operation of a single helicopter – typically a Ka-27PS/Ka-28

Previous page: The Project 21301 flight deck is located on the bow section. Above: A Project 18270 rescue vehicle alongside a Project 21301 mothership. Admiralty Shipyards

Page 43: Project 18270 DSRV. Above: A Project 18270 DSRV being positioned over the docking hatch of a Russian submarine. USC

The decision to equip the Pacific Fleet with Bester DSRV's was formalised in January 2016. As the Project 21301 Salvage and Rescue Vessel *Igor Belousov* was not yet available it was decided to equip the rescue vessel *Alagez* with Bester prior to the *Igor Belousov* becoming available. The first of the Bester vehicles arrived at Vladivostok, Russian Far East, in early January 2016 (MODRF, 2016). The *Igor Belousov* conducted navigation tests in the Baltic before proceeding to Vladivostok to join the 79th Rescue Detachment of the Russian Pacific Fleet (MODRF, 2016).

Bester has been employed on multinational rescue exercises involving the Russian Federation Navy and China's PLAN (Peoples Liberation Army Navy), notably in September 2017 (MODRF, 2017), as those nations forged closer military ties in the face of perceived threats from western alliances. This training operation involved ships and helicopters – Ka-27PS (Russian Navy) and Z-9Z and Z-9D shipborne helicopters (PLAN).

The Bester/Project 21301 capability assisted in the search in the South Atlantic for the Argentine Navy submarine, *San Juan* that contact had been lost with on 15 November 2017 (MODRF, 2017). The Project 21301 vessel *Yantar* moved from the West African coast and operated in support of the operation from 6 December 2017 until 1 April 2018. Although the Bester DSRV was not employed in its rescue role, prior to the operation being ended the Russian detachment conducted six descents by ROV to depths ranging from 126 m to 970 m in response to detection contacts, which proved not be the missing submarine (MODRF, 2017).

Russian Littoral Submarines & Submersibles

Page 45-47: Project 18270 Bester/Project 21301 – Russian Federation Pacific Fleet – rescue exercise in Peter the Great Gulf, employing a Project 877 diesel electric submarine as a simulated vessel in distress. MODRF

Project 18270 deep sea rescue vehicle operations. Admiralty Shipyards/MODRF

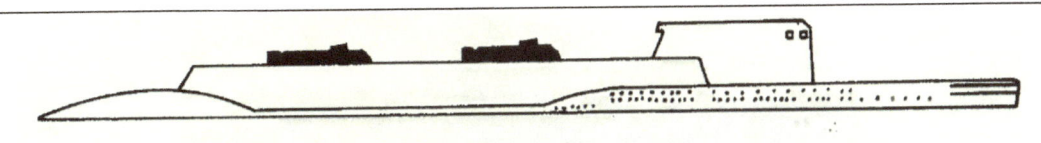

Top: US DIA artist depiction of a Soviet India Class (Project 940) submarine launching DSRV's, one of which is docking with a disabled Project 627 submarine on the sea floor. Centre: Crude starboard side on profile of an intelligence assessment of the India Class. Above: A photograph taken by a USN maritime patrol aircraft showing an India Class submarine on the surface with two DSRV'S in their semi-recessed stowed position atop the hull. US DIA/US DoD

The Project 940 Lenok (NATO reporting name 'India'), was a two boat class designed to accommodate DSRV for underwater rescue operations. While the Project 940 DSRV carriers have long since been retired the Russian Federation Navy still operates the Project 18551 deep sea rescue submersible from surface ship platforms, notably the *Kommuna* (*Commune*), which was still in operation with the Black Sea Fleet in 2019 (MODRF). The *Kommuna* had initially entered service with the Baltic Fleet of the Imperial Russian Navy on 15 July 1915. The ship had been laid down on 12 November 1912 and launched on 17 November 1913. This vessel was involved in a submarine salvage operation as far back as 1917, when it raised the submarine AG-15 near the Aland Islands at the entrance to the Gulf of Finland. The vessel served through WW I and WW II in the Baltic Sea, continued to serve through the Cold War and was transferred from Kronstadt in the Baltic to Sevastopol, Crimea, to serve with the Soviet Black Sea Fleet. The *Kommuna* underwent modernisation to equip it with modern rescue equipment, including the AS-26 submersible (MODRF).

Although not a submersible, it would be prudent to briefly detail the capabilities of the Russian Navy rescue diving bell, SC-64, operating with several vessels, including the Rescue Ship *Epron* of the Black Sea Fleet. The SC-64 has accommodation for two crew and eight rescued personnel and can be used to dry dock with a submarine at depths down to 500 m (MODRF, 2017).

While the Project 18270 Bester is the main deep sea rescue vehicle being promoted by Russia in 2019, there have been a number of such vehicles available for civil and military rescue and engineering/survey work over the previous several decades. Some have been retired, while the status of others is hazy at best. The Project 18551 deep sea rescue vehicle, AC-28 (above) remains in service in 2019. Krsormovo

Page 51-53: The Black Sea rescue ship *Commune* with the Project 18551 deep sea rescue vehicle, AC-28. The image above shows the *Commune* in the Black Sea on 6 December 2018, with the AC-28 in the foreground. MODRF

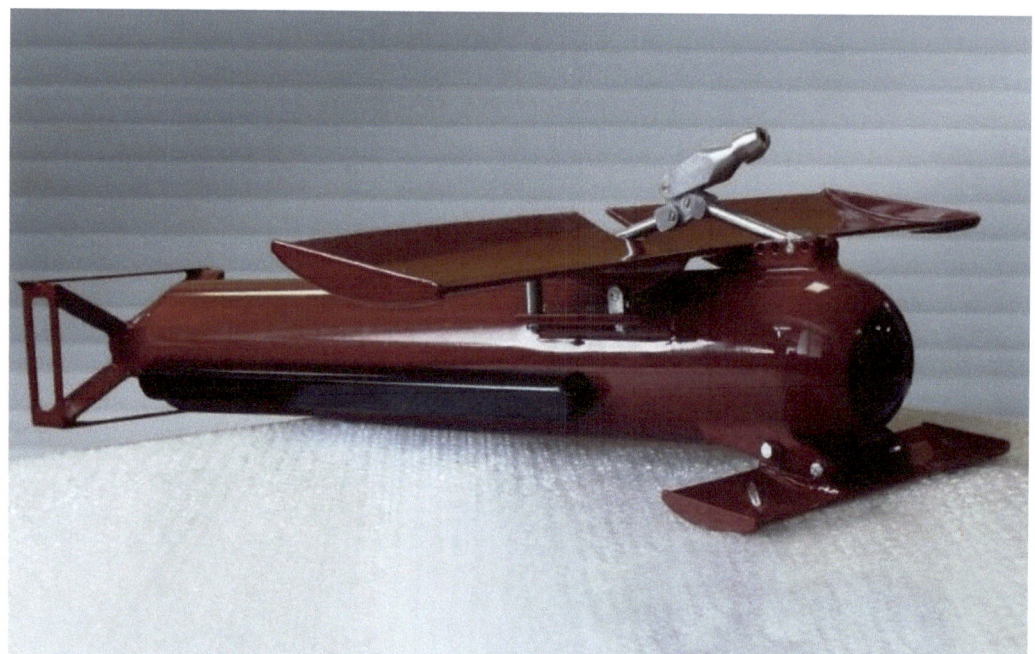

This graphic (above) depicts a Project 21301 Salvage and Rescue Vessel employing a mine hunting and bottom object detection sonar system (illustrated top), which is designed to detect and classify moored sea mines and objects, such as a disabled submarine, on the sea bottom. *Aquamarin*

4

TOURIST SUBMARINES (SUBMERSIBLES)

It is, perhaps, pertinent to mention one other family of Russian submersibles operating in a civil capacity, this line commencing with the *Neptune* tourist submarine (submersible). The *Neptune* was designed and built in the last years of the Soviet Union, design work having commenced at CDB ME-Rubin in 1988. The vessel, which was completed in 1989, was built at Sevmashpredpriyatie, the work being completed in 1991. Following completion of trials the vessel was operated as a tourist submarine from Antigua Island in the Lesser Antilles for several years before being returned to Russia for overhaul and enhancement to systems.

The success of the *Neptune* in operation led to another vessel, the electric propulsion *Sadko*, which was designed at CDB ME-Rubin under Chief Designer Y.N. Kormilitsin. This vessel, which was built in co-operation with JSC Bars at JSC Petrozavod (Petrozavodsk) in St. Petersburg, Russia, was launched on 25 June 1997, and, following a program of trials, was transferred to and operated from Saint Lucia Island in the Lesser Antilles from June 1998 until August 2000. The *Sadko* was transferred to Cyprus in 2001. In the second decade of the twenty first century the vessel is reported by JSC Bars as still being based in Larnaca, Cyprus.

The *Sadko*, which has a length of 30 m, width, 4.5 m, weight, 170 tons and can submerge to a depth of 60 m (JSC Bars), was built to comply with international safety standards for such vessels. The vessel incorporated additional features, exceeding the international standard for safety of the boats hull and major structural components, such as the side portholes. The sustainer propulsion consisted of 4 x submersible electric motors and 4 x independent thrusters, allowing for ease of navigation through the water. The vessel demonstrated positive buoyancy in all cruise regimes. The incorporation of electric drives allowed to forgo hydraulics in an attempt to reduce adverse effects on the environment during operation. The boat was designed with excellent manoeuvrability, which allowed for conducting operations that had minimum effect on 'flora and fauna' (CDB ME-Rubin).

The *Sadko* tourist submarine (submersible) has a length of 30 m, width, 4.5 m, weighs 170 tons and can submerge to a depth of 60 m. CDB ME-Rubin

JSC Bars is, in the second decade of the twenty first century, designing modern tourist submarines along the lines of the *Sadko*, with the capacity to produce several boats simultaneously if orders are forthcoming. The design house is also involved in other areas of civil submersible design, typified by its Golubooy Kosmos (Blue Space) two-person underwater vehicle, featuring 'combined muscular' (manual cycling) and electric drive motor (JSC Bars). The design, developed by the Marine Technical University, has a length of 3.5 m, width, 2.7 m, height, 1.2 m, weighs up to 2000 kg (in operating condition) and can submerge to depths down to 25 m at submerged speeds up to 3 knots (JSC Bars). Small tourist submarines (submersibles) that can submerse to a depth of 50 m are, in the second decade of the twenty first century, being promoted by Russia's CDB Lazurit.

Computer generated graphic of a tourist submarine, developed from the *Sadko* design, being promoted by JSC Bars in the second decade of the twenty first century. Bars

Previous page: The tourism submarine (submersible) *Sadko* under construction at JSC Bars. This page top: The *Sadko* being prepared for launch. Above: The *Sadko* during sea trials. Bars

This page top: The two-person Underwater Vehicle Golubooy Kosmos (Blue Space) submersible, which was being promoted by **JSC Bars** in 2019. Above: A tourist submarine (submersible) design being promoted by **CDB Lazurit**. JSC Bars/CDB Lazurit

6

SUBMARINE SYSTEMS & ARMAMENT

Modern submarines are controlled by a complex that provides automatic and remote automated control of the vessels general purpose systems and the diesel generators auxiliary system overseeing various operations. This includes submerging and surfacing operations and overseeing elements of the reloading operation for the torpedo/missile armament, among other functions. In the Project 636 large diesel electric submarine this complex is the JSC Avora Scientific and Production Association Palladij-M (Avora). It is unclear, in 2018, if a variant of this complex is incorporated into the small size littoral attack submarine designs. A complex is incorporated to provide control of the three-dimensional motion of the submarine, on the sea surface or submerged, through synergy of control surfaces, such as rudders. Other systems may include a KADK, or a variation, which provides the host submarine with 'generation and indication of static list and trim angles… in submerged position' (Avora).

The littoral attack submarines can be equipped with a multi-functional hierarchical combat information and control system with capabilities along the lines of the Lama-EKM AICS (Automated Information and Control System), which entered production in 1999. Such systems can oversee routine submarine operations and complex combat operations through control of the torpedo/missile launchers and the transfer mission profile data into the weapons (Avora).

There has, in 2019, been no release of information as regards to sonar equipment fit for the small size littoral attack submarine designs, but it is expected that the inhabited submersibles would be equipped with either a variation of the JSC Concern Okeanpribor (Oceanpribor) Coelacanth sonar designed for such vehicles, or a similar system. As they are not in serial production the specific sensor suites of the littoral attack submarines of the Piranha-T, P-550 and P-650E designs remain open. The various suites would be installed according to customer specification. There are a number of options that could build on the Oceanpribor developed MGK-400EM installed in the Project 636 or the 'Lira' large-array antenna sonar technology installed in the Project 677 in service with the Russian Federation Navy.

A brief discussion, utlising data furnished by JSC Concern Okeanpribor (Oceanpribor) and Rosoboronexport, of the functions of the MGK-400EM sonar, which includes modern antennas featuring piezoelectric ceramic compounds and electroacoustic transducers, will serve to demonstrate the type of capability that may be expected in the littoral attack submarines. The sonar is designed to provide the host submarine with accurate surveys of the surface and sub-surface environments and warning of any navigational hazards and coastlines in the vicinity, as well as provide the relevant targeting data to the submarine weapons systems. The main functions of the system are to detect surface and sub-surface targets, which includes ships, submarines and weapons, such as torpedoes, all of which are detected by the acoustic signature (the noisier a target is then the easier it would be to detect); automatic tracking of ship, submarine and torpedo targets; ELINT (Electronic Intelligence) through the interception of the signals that are emitted by active sonar on various platforms – ships, submarines and torpedoes; detection of sub-surface submarine targets in active mode; ranging to a target submarine being tracked in a listening mode; detection of navigational obstacles and moored mines when operating in the active mode; exchanging of data with other systems through the use of a hydro-acoustic channel and target identification of surface ships and sub-surface targets, such as submarines and torpedoes, ship, submarine and torpedo targets being classified in the passive (listening mode); the transfer of the basic targeting information to the submarine information combat management system to allow weapons to be targeted; measuring the hydro-acoustic levels of interference with the sonar system; range prediction and display of detected targets; diagnostics and automated testing of the system and recommendations for fixing problems.

In 360° listening mode, a complex in the class of the MGK-400EM can detect a submarine target generating a 0.05 Pa/Hz noise signature at a range out to 16 km. A surface vessel generating a 10 Pa/Hz noise signature would be detected at a range out to 100 km. Up to 12 targets could be automatically tracked simultaneously within a bearing accuracy of 10 arm min. In Hydro-location mode the complex can scan ± 30° out to a range of 16 km for various target sets. Threats such as a moored sea mine can be detected at around 1.8 km – depending on target size.

The stable of littoral submarines being marketed in Russia would employ a unified periscope system along the lines of, but not necessarily, the PARUS-98E unified periscope system developed by JSC Concern CSRI Elektropribor, State Research Centre of the Russian Federation. This system, which consists of an attack periscope, which penetrates into the hull, and a multipurpose (optronic mast), which does not penetrate the submarine hull, provides the host platform with 24 hour surveillance capability in all-weather conditions; GPS (Global Positioning System) signal reception and radar signal detection. The various components are separate from each other and can be fitted to submarines in concert or as separate items of equipment in concert with other masts and systems (Elektropribor).

The small size submarines would be equipped with a communications system such as the CSRI Elektropribor developed DISTANCIA-E. This system is intended for medium/large submarines down to small submarines of the Piranha, Piranha-T, P-550 and P-650E designs. The communications system, which allows vessels to retain touch with coastal command centres as well as other command centres, such as shipborne and airborne, can receive VLF, LF, MF and HF waveband radio signals intercepted by the antenna on a towed buoyant cable whilst the submarine is submerged. On the surface, or at periscope depth, radio signals can be received on VLF, LF, MF, HF and VHF frequency bands on the extendable antenna and on a crossed-loop antenna. Satellite communications can be received in an IMMARSAT-C system. The host submarine can also receive Omega and Loran-C shore navigation system signals when surfaced or at when at periscope depth (Elektropribor).

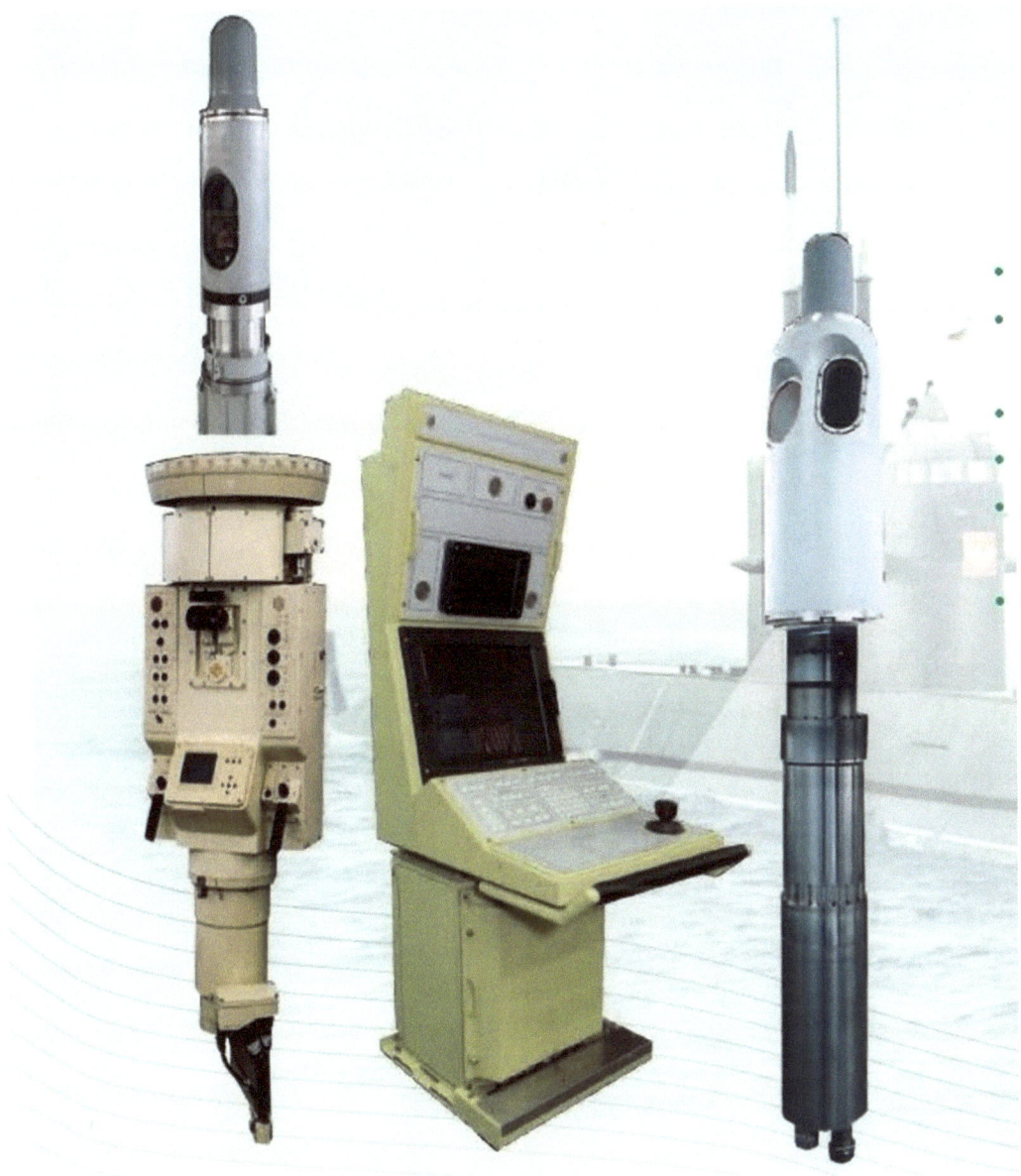

PARUS-98E Unified Periscope System. Elektropribor

Another system available for the littoral submarine designs is the Elektropribor, developed APPASSIONATA-E miniature navigation complex. This system comprises a miniature INS (Inertial Navigation System), gyrocompass, log and echo sounder, receptors for satellite and radio navigation systems, a magnetic compass and generates navigational data, not only for the submarine itself, but also for the weapons systems and other onboard systems. Navigational data can be generated when the host platform is travelling at speeds up to 20 knots (Elektropribor).

Modern Russian submarines and surface warship designs can be equipped with an inertial navigation and stabilisation system such as the Elektropribor LADOGA-ME, which provides the host vessels with navigation and stabilisation parameters (Elektropribor). Others systems that can be incorporated include the K-697E floating (retractable) trailing (700 m cable) antenna device, developed by Elektropribor. The K-697E, which provides submerged submarines with the ability to transmit and receive VLF, LF, MF and HF signals, can receive signals in the following frequency ranges: VLF and LF – 6-150 KHz; MF and HF – 0.13-30 MHz. VLF and LF signals can be received when the submarine is submerged at depths of 60-100 m and MF and HF signals can be received at submerged depths of 50-85 m whilst the submarine is travelling at speeds of between 2.5-4 knots. The towing speed upper limit for the deployed antenna is 20 knots, with the capability for short term speeds up to 25 knots (Elektropribor). A floating emergency information complex would be incorporated, such as the V-603E, which transmits COSPAS-SARSAT SOS signals if the submarine is in distress.

Modern Russian diesel electric submarines can be armed with a plethora of weapons – torpedoes, mines and cruise missiles. The littoral attack submarines can be equipped with such weapons, allowing them to engage surface and sub-surface naval targets and fixed land targets. The baseline armament for modern diesel-electric, as well as nuclear powered, attack submarines and the small size littoral attack submarine designs, remains the humble torpedo, which in its modern guise remains an effective weapon for use against surface and sub-surface targets. The main types of torpedo available for the small size littoral submarines are the TE-2 and UGST (Universal Wake Homing Torpedo) 533 mm class weapons and the MTT 400 mm class weapon.

The TE-2 electrically-driven remotely controlled 533 mm calibre class homing torpedo is designed to engage submarines and warships in motion as well as fixed targets, such as stationary vessels and maritime installations. Whilst the weapon can be employed by surface warships in the autonomous mode only, it can be launched from submarines in both remotely controlled and autonomous modes. The weapon is designed for employment in a wide range of oceanic/sea conditions, ranging from water salinity of 30-35 pro mille and temperature ranges of 0° to +25° C. It incorporates what is described as a three-beam anti-ship homing system and forgoes a proximity acoustic exploder, which is substituted by an active influence electromagnetic exploder with the capability of attacking underwater targets (Rosoboronexport).

TE-2-01 (top) and UGST (above) homing torpedoes. Rosoboronexport

There are three variants of the TE-2 available for operations from submarines and surface warships. The TE-2-01 features mechanical data inputs, the TE-2-02 features the ability to receive electrical data inputs through a UKASTU unified shipborne remote control system and the TE-2-03 features performance improvements over the earlier variants, as well as incorporating the function of electric data inputs through the UKASTU.

Length values for a live torpedo with command wire are 8188 mm for the TE-2-01, 8300 mm for the TE-2-02 and 8100 mm for the TE-2-03. Length values for a live torpedo, minus command wire, are 7863 mm for the TE-2-01/02 and 7650 mm for the TE-2-03. All three variants, which are armed with a 250 kg weight warhead, have an overall weight value of 2400 kg with command wire and 2350 kg without command wire. Engagement range for all three variants is 15000 m in first mode and 25000 m in second mode for the TE-2-01/02, increasing to 30000 m for the TE-2-03. Average speed values for the TE-2-01/02, when operating at maximum range in water 'with a 35 pro milli salinity…' is 45±2 knots, increasing to 48±2 knots for the TE-2-03 in first mode. Speed values in second mode are 32±3 knots for the TE-2-01/02. Submersed targets can be engaged at depths of 20-450 m with the TE-2-01/02 increasing to 20-600 m for the TE-2-03 (Rosoboronexport).

The UGST 533 mm calibre class weapon was developed in the 1990's as a replacement for the Type 53-65 torpedo. Operating speed is 50 knots (Mode 1) or 35 knots (Mode 2). The weapon can engage targets a depths from 8-500 m out to a range of 40 km, with an enhanced ability to defeat defensive countermeasures. Basic characteristics include a length of 7.2 m and weight values of 2200 kg for the torpedo and 300 kg for the warhead (Rosoboronexport).

MTT – A small-size thermal torpedo, the MTT, was developed as an ASW (Anti-Submarine Warfare) torpedo for deployment on Russian designed surface warships and submarines. The weapon consists of six main sections – 'equipment module; warhead section; adaption section; fuel tank section; power section; tail unit' (Rosoboronexport). The torpedo is powered by a piston engine consuming 'pronit-type high-energy single component fuel' (Rosoboronexport). The high power of this engine/fuel combination allows the MTT to be employed against a range of high speed targets – the major design driver being to destroy modern nuclear powered submarines. The equipment fit consist of an advanced homing system overseen by an onboard computer system. The MTT is capable of tracking several (number unspecified) targets in a number of engagement modes at depths ranging from 8 m down to 500 m when operating in an environment of sonar countermeasures (Rosoboronexport). The warhead section accommodated the directional explosive charge designed to kill submarines of modern design.

The 324 mm (400 mm class) calibre MTT characteristics included: length, 3200 mm; weight, up to 390 kg; explosive weight, up to 60 kg; two speed modes, 50±1.5 knots, mode 1 and 30±1.5 knots, mode 2; maximum range, 9 km, mode 1 and 20 km, mode 2; running depth and target engagement depth, 15-600 m; minimum water depth for host submarine, 40 m; homing system acquisition range (submarine target with a radius of 3-4 m operating at a speed of 3-35 knots), 2.5 km at water depths below 200 m and 1.5 km at water depths of 40-200 m (Rosoboronexport).

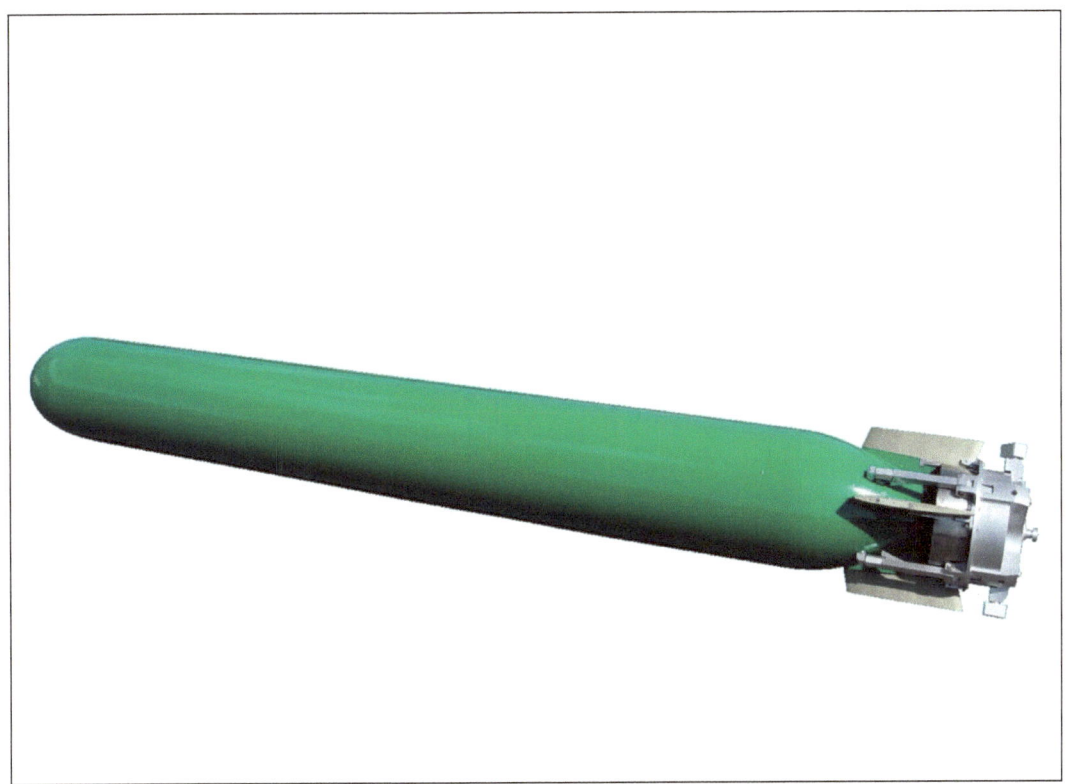

Top: MTT small-size thermal torpedo. Above: JSC Experimental Machine Design Bureau, Novator graphic depicting the full range of missiles available for the Club-S missile complex. Rosoboronexport/Novator

Club-S was designed as a submarine launched variant of the surface launched Club-N integrated cruise missile complex, both variants designed to operate against surface vessels and submarines in an environment active and passive countermeasures. Club-S/N is a unified combat system comprising two separate types of anti-ship cruise missile and an anti-submarine ballistic missile. The 3M-54E anti-ship cruise missile of the Club-S system includes a booster section, a low-altitude subsonic sustainer and a separable supersonic warhead section. The 3M-54E1 anti-ship cruise missile consists of a booster stage and a low-altitude subsonic sustainer. The 91RE1 anti-submarine ballistic missile element of the Club-S complex includes an MPT-1UME high speed homing torpedo that separates from the missile body following the flight to the target area.

The Club-S complex incorporates an automated fire control system that operates in real-time utilising target data provided by the submarine sensors through the combat information management system, or, by direct manual input and through the use of navigational data. Missiles of the Club-S complex can be launched from standard 533 mm class torpedo tubes after the system calculates the launch data and oversees the pre-launch and launch procedures.

The anti-ship variants are equipped with a modern INS to guide them to the target area where a jam-resistant active radar seeker takes over for the terminal phase of the attack. The 91RE1 anti-submarine ballistic missile element of the Club-S complex is guided to the target area by the onboard INS, the MPT-1UME homing torpedo, after separation and immersion in the water, being guided to the target by the onboard sonar/target seeker (Rosoboronexport & Novator).

The 3M-14E LACM (Land Attack Cruise Missile) is offered as an export option enhancement to the Club-S complex. This weapon can strike land targets with a 450 kg warhead at distances ranging from 10-275 km.

Technical Specification Club-S Missile Complex – data furnished by Rosoboronexport			
	3M-54E	3M-54E1	91RE1
Length:	8.220 m	6.2 m	7.65 m
Diameter:	0.534 m	0.534 m	0.534 m
Weight:	2275 kg	1754 kg	2100 kg
Warhead weight:	200 kg	200 kg	76 kg
Operational range:	10-220 km	10-275 km	5-50 km
Sustainer speed:	180-240 m/s (Mach 0.6-0.8)	180-240 m/s (Mach 0.6-0.8)	830 m/s
Guidance system:	INS + active radar seeker		united
	inertial+		
			acoustic
	target		
			seeker
Trajectory:	all three variants - low altitude ballistic		

Technical specification for 3M-14E LACM – data furnished by Rosoboronexport

Length: 6200 mm
Diameter: 534 mm
Launch weight: 1696 kg
Warhead weight: 450 kg
Operational range: 10-275 km
Sustainer portion flight speed: 180-240 m/s
Guidance system: Doppler/inertial + inertial GPS (GLONASS)

Among the various mines that can be employed are the MDM-1 sea bottom mine and the PMK-2 ASW mine, both of which are deployed from the submarine torpedo tubes. Both the MDM-1 and the PMK-2 can be deployed automatically from the 533 mm class torpedo tubes by submarines travelling at speeds up to 8 knots. The MDM-1 Mod.1 is intended to destroy or damage surface vessels and submarines, the latter either surfaced or submerged. The three channel influence exploders can be activated by a target vessels acoustic, electromagnetic and hydrodynamic signatures (Rosoboronexport).

MDM-1 Mod.1, Sea Mine – data furnished by Rosoboronexport

Diameter: 533 mm class (534 mm)
Length: 2860 mm
Weight: 960 kg
Operating depth: 8-120 m
Service life once planted: 1 year

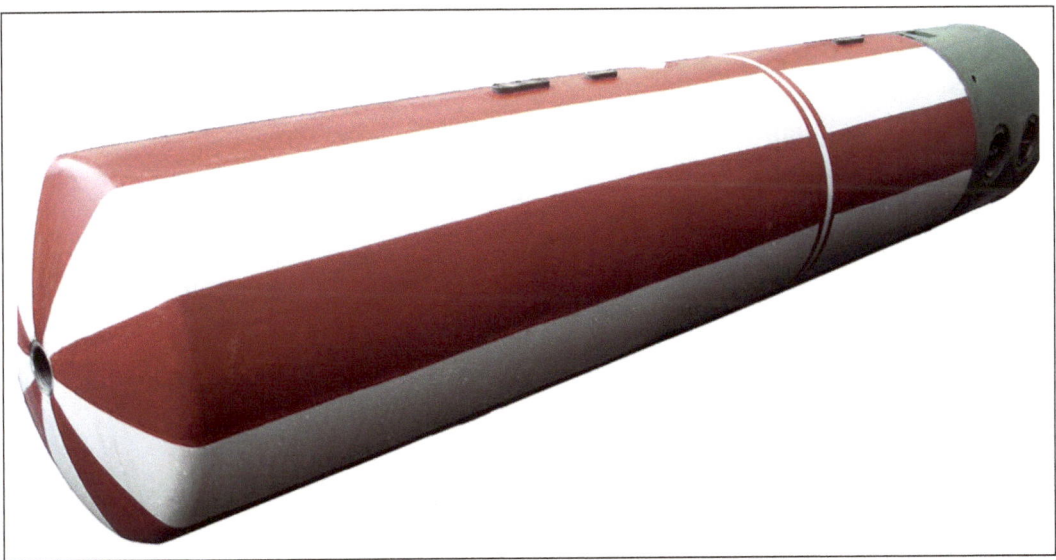

MDM-1 Mod.1 Sea Mine. Rosoboronexport

The PMK-2 is deployed at preset depths, targets being detected and acquired by the onboard sonar, which then designates the target, allowing it to be engaged by the onboard small size ASW torpedo. Once launched, the torpedo swims a circuitous pattern as it searches for the target submarine, the homing system then locking-on and guiding the weapon to the target, which is destroyed by the 130 kg class high explosive warhead activated by a combination fuse (Rosoboronexport).

> PMK-2 ASW Mine System – data furnished by Rosoboronexport
>
> **Diameter:** 533 mm class
> **Length:** 5600-7900 mm
> **Weight:** 1400-1800 kg
> **TNT equivalent warhead weight:** 130 kg
> **Planting depth:** 100-1000 m
> **Operational life once planted:** 1 year, after which it self-destructs

Graphic depicting a Russian small size submarine of the Piranha-T type conducting the full spectrum of combat tasking's of Russian conventional submarines – engaging enemy submarine with torpedo, engaging enemy surface warship with 3M-54E(1) anti-ship cruise missile, engaging land target with 3M-14E land attack cruise missile, deploying a row of seabed mines and deploying teams of combat swimmers for reconnaissance and or to attack targets in littoral waters, including offshore structures. Malachite

GLOSSARY

Arc min	Arc minute (unit of angular measurement. 1 arm minute = 60 arc seconds and 3600 arc seconds = 1 arc degree, one 360th of a complete circle
ASW	Anti-Submarine Warfare
DoD	Department of Defence
DSRV	Deep Sea Rescue Vehicle
ELINT	Electronic Intelligence
GLONASS	Globanaya Navigozionnaya Sputnikovaya Sistema (Global Navigation Satellite System)
HF	High Frequency
INS	Inertial Navigation System
JEPS	Joint Electrical Power System
JSC	Joint Stock Company
KHz	Kilohertz
Km	Kilometer
Knots	Nautical Miles
kW	Kilowatt
LACM	Land Attack Cruise Missile
LF	Low Frequency
m	Metre
m^3	Meter Cubed
Mach	Mach 1 = Speed of Sound. Varies with altitude
MAD	Magnetic Anomaly Detection
MF	Medium Frequency
mm	Millimetre
MODRF	Ministry of Defence of the Russian Federation
NATO	North Atlantic Treaty Organisation
PJSC	Public Joint Stock Company
PLAN	Peoples Liberation Army Navy
UGST	Universal Wake Homing Torpedo
US	United States
USC	United Shipbuilding Corporation
USN	United States Navy
USSR	Union of Soviet Socialist Republics
VLF	Very Low Frequency
x	Times (multiplication)
±	Plus or minus
~	Approximately equal to (can also be used to mean asymptotically equal)
°	Degree

ABOUT THE AUTHOR

Hugh Harkins FRAS is a historian and author with an extensive research background in astro/geophysics and studies/research in the wider scientific, aeronautic, astronautic and nautical technical and historical fields. He is also involved in research in the field of Scottish history, which formed a significant element of an otherwise scientific undergraduate degree. Hugh has published in excess of sixty books; non-fiction and fiction, writing under his given name as well as utilising several pseudonyms. He has also written for several international magazines, whilst his work has been used as reference for many other projects, ranging from the aviation industry, international news corporations and film media to encyclopaedias, museum exhibits and the computer gaming industry. Hugh is a member of the Institute of Physics and is an elected Fellow of the Royal Astronomical Society. He currently resides in his native Scotland. Other titles by the author include:

Russia's Coastal Missile Shield - Bal-E & Bastion Mobile Coastal Cruise Missile Complexes
Iskander - Mobile Tactical Aero-Ballistic/Cruise Missile Complex
Orbital/Fractional Orbit Bombardment System - The Soviet Globalnaya Raketa
Counter-Space Defence Co-Orbital Satellite Fighter
Russia's Strategic Missile Carrier/Bomber Roadmap 2018-2040 – PAK DA, Tu-160M2, Tu-95MSM & Tu-22M3M
Sukhoi T-50/PAK FA - Russia's 5th Generation 'Stealth' Fighter
Sukhoi Su-35S 'Flanker' E - Russia's 4++ Generation Super-Manoeuvrability Fighter
Sukhoi Su-34 'Fullback'
Sukhoi Su-30MKK/MK2/M2 - Russo Kitashiy Striker from Amur
Soviet Mixed Power Experimental Fighter Aircraft – Piston-Liquid Propellant Rocket Engine/Piston-Ramjet/Piston-Pulsejet & Piston-Compressor Jet Engine Designs of the 1940's
MiG-35/D 'Fulcrum' F – Towards the Fifth Generation
Air War over Syria, Tu-160, Tu-95MS & Tu-22M3 - Cruise Missile and Bombing Strikes on Syria, November 2015-February 2016
Sukhoi Su-27SM(3)/SKM
Russian/Soviet Aircraft Carrier & Carrier Aviation Design & Evolution Volume 1 - Seaplane Carriers, Project 71/72, Graf Zeppelin, Project 1123 ASW Cruiser & Project 1143-1143.4
Heavy Aircraft Carrying Cruiser
Light Battle Cruisers and the Second Battle of Heligoland Bight
British Battlecruisers of World War 1 - Operational Log, July 1914-June 1915
Eurofighter Typhoon - Storm over Europe
North American F-108 Rapier - Mach 3 Interceptor
Convair YB-60 - Fort Worth Overcast
Boeing X-36 Tailless Agility Flight Research Aircraft
X-32 - The Boeing Joint Strike Fighter
X-35 - Progenitor to the F-35 Lightning II
X-45 Uninhabited Combat Air Vehicle
Into The Cauldron - The Lancaster MK.I Daylight Raid on Augsburg
Hurricane IIB Combat Log - 151 Wing RAF, North Russia 1941
RAF Meteor Jet Fighters in World War II, an Operational Log
Typhoon IA/B Combat Log - Operation Jubilee, August 1942
Defiant MK.I Combat Log - Fighter Command, May-September 1940
Blenheim MK.IF Combat Log - Fighter Command Day Fighter Sweeps/Night Interceptions, September 1939 - June 1940
Fortress MK.I Combat Log - Bomber Command High Altitude Bombing Operations, July-September 1941

www.ingramcontent.com/pod-product-compliance
Lightning Source LLC
Chambersburg PA
CBHW042021150426
43197CB00003B/91